Smithsonian

SHARKS!

Brenda Scott Royce

Contents

SHARKS

Sharks are among the world's most fascinating creatures.

Sharks are a type of fish. Like other fish, sharks swim by moving their bodies from side to side. Sharks need to swim in order to live. They get the oxygen they need from the water around them.

? DID YOU KNOW?

More than four hundred species of sharks live in the ocean. Each shark species has special features that make it unique.

At Home in the Ocean

Sharks are found in all of the world's oceans. They live in the deep dark ocean and in shallow coastal waters.

The Earth's oceans are all connected, and many sharks **migrate**, or travel long distances, in search of food or mates. Seasonal changes in water temperature are one reason sharks migrate. Blacktip sharks move south along the east coast of the United States every winter, seeking warmer waters.

Most sharks
prefer warm waters,
but Greenland sharks make
their home near the North Pole!
These huge, slow-moving sharks inhabit the icy
waters of the Arctic and North Atlantic Oceans.

Bull sharks are one of the few shark species that can survive in fresh water for long periods of time. Bull sharks have been known to travel long distances up rivers, including the Amazon, the Mississippi, and the Ganges.

Built to Swim

Sharks are ideally suited to a life at sea. Most have torpedo-shaped bodies that help them easily glide through water. A shark's powerful tail propels it forward. Its fins are used for steering and keeping the shark steady.

Sharks don't have bones; their skeletons are made of **cartilage**. Cartilage is lighter and more flexible than bone.

Shark's skeletons are made of the same material as human noses and ears.

? DID YOU KNOW?

Sharks get the oxygen they need from the water around them. Depending on the species, a shark has five to seven pairs of **gills**. These slit-like openings pull oxygen from the water. Most sharks breathe by swimming with their mouths open, which allows water to pass through their gills.

great white shark's gills

Shark skin appears smooth, but if you rub it the wrong way it feels like sandpaper. That's because shark skin is covered with tiny structures called **dermal denticles**. Dermal denticles are covered with enamel, just like human teeth, making shark skin very tough.
By channeling water, dermal denticles also increase a shark's swimming speed!

Tons of Teeth

Sharks produce new teeth throughout their entire lives. If a shark loses a tooth, they will replace it. In fact, they have rows of teeth waiting in line.

Some sharks lose up to thirty thousand teeth in their lifetime. A great white shark has three thousand teeth in its mouth at all times.

DID YOU KNOW?

Venice, Florida, is known as the "shark's tooth capital of the world" due to the large number of shark teeth that wash up on its sandy beaches every year.

Sharks are often feared because of their many sharp teeth. But not all sharks have large, razor-like teeth.

Whale sharks have rows of tiny teeth. They use their teeth like a rake to sift food from the water.

The flattened back teeth of horn sharks are great for crushing the shells of clams, crabs, snails, and other prey.

All Shapes and Sizes

Sharks come in many shapes and sizes.

The grey reef shark has the familiar torpedo shape that most people associate with sharks.

The angel shark is wide and flat.

A thresher shark's enormous curved tail takes up one-third of its body weight.

The whale shark is bigger than a schoolbus.

The pygmy dogshark is smaller than a shoebox.

How do these sharks stack up?

whale shark: 40 feet

great white: 20 feet

hammerhead: 13 feet

tiger shark: 10 feet

zebra shark: 9 feet

shortfin mako: 7 feet

frilled shark: 6 feet

tasseled wobbegong: 5½ feet

leopard shark: 4 feet

horn shark: 3 feet

cookie-cutter shark: 20 inches

pygmy dogshark: 7 inches

? DID YOU KNOW?

In most shark species, females are larger than males.

Killer Fish

The great white shark is one of the most feared and aggressive sharks on the planet. It is an **apex predator**, the top of its **food chain**; no other animals eat it.

?DID YOU KNOW? Great white sharks have incredible senses that help them locate prey. They can detect blood from three miles away!

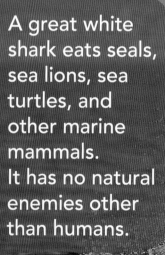

A great white shark eats seals, sea lions, sea turtles, and other marine mammals. It has no natural enemies other than humans.

Great white sharks are found in oceans around the world. They go on long migrations to look for food.

One great white shark traveled from South Africa to Australia and back—a distance of more than thirteen thousand miles—in about nine months. Scientists named this long-distance swimmer "Nicole" after actress Nicole Kidman, a shark fan.

Indian Ocean

South Africa

Australia

Gentle Giant

The whale shark is the biggest fish in the world. It can weigh more than forty thousand pounds.

Despite their name, whale sharks are gentle giants rather than fierce predators. They feed mainly on plankton and small fish. Plankton are tiny organisms that drift in the ocean. The whale shark swims along with its massive mouth open and just sucks them in.

? DID YOU KNOW?

A whale shark's mouth can be five feet wide— almost large enough for a small car to drive through!

Whale sharks have polka-dotted backs. Just as no two human fingerprints are the same, each whale shark has a unique pattern of spots. Scientists use special software to help identify an individual whale shark by its markings. This software was first developed by NASA to map the stars!

Whale sharks spend most of their time alone. But they sometimes gather in huge groups of hundreds of whale sharks to feed. Thanks to the whale shark's peaceful personality, scientists can observe these animals up close without danger.

Looks Like...

It's easy to see how these sharks got their names.

Hammerhead

This shark's unusual head, shaped somewhat like a hammer, is used to trap stingrays by pinning them down. Stingrays are the hammerhead's favorite food.

The hammerhead's eyes are at the ends of its head, allowing it to see all around, even above and below. It cannot, however, see straight ahead!

Bonnethead

The bonnethead, a member of the hammerhead family, has a rounded head. Its head is shaped like a woman's bonnet or a shovel blade (which is why bonnetheads are sometimes called shovelhead sharks).

Sawshark

This shark's snout looks like the blade of a chainsaw. The sawshark uses its saw to dig prey out of sandy sea bottoms. It will also move its head rapidly from side to side to slash at prey.

Sawsharks and sawfish look a lot alike—but only one of these animals is a shark. Sawfish are members of the ray family, along with stingrays and manta rays. The sawshark's barbels—a pair of whisker-like protrusions on the snout—are one way to tell them apart.

sawfish

Spots and Stripes

Tiger Shark)))))

The vertical stripes on young tiger sharks give this species its name. When the shark grows up, its stripes will fade or disappear. These aggressive sharks have sharp, curved teeth, which allow them to rip through the shells of sea turtles. They also eat other sharks, sea birds, and sea mammals.

Zebra Shark)))))

The zebra shark has stripes like a zebra when it is born. Like the tiger shark, the zebra shark loses its stripes when it reaches adulthood. Adult zebra sharks have spots instead of stripes.

baby zebra shark

Leopard Shark

Like a leopard found in a forest, the leopard shark is covered in spots. Because their mouths are located on the undersides of their heads, they can eat crabs, clams, and fish eggs as they swim along the ocean floor. The leopard shark's spots serve as camouflage, helping it blend in with its surroundings.

adult zebra shark

Weird and Wonderful

One of the strangest shark species on the planet, the cookie-cutter shark gets its name from its odd style of eating. It bites with its pointy lower teeth then spins its body around, slicing a circular chunk of flesh off a prey animal.

? DID YOU KNOW?

These small sharks have been known to attack animals much larger than themselves— including great white sharks!

With fringes that resemble seaweed, the tasseled wobbegong is a master of disguise. This odd-looking bottom-dweller blends right in with coral reefs and algae-covered rocks. When a fish swims within reach, the wobbegong opens its large mouth and sucks it in.

The bramble shark has thorny scales covering its body.

Can a shark glow in the dark? Tiny organs called photophores on the lanternshark's skin produce light.

The epaulette shark can swim, but it mainly moves by "walking" on the ocean bottom, using its fins as legs!

21

Shark Records

BIGGEST:

At more than forty feet long, the whale shark easily wins the prize for the biggest fish in the sea.

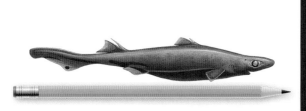

At about six inches in length, the dwarf lanternshark is most likely the world's smallest shark.

fastest:

The shortfin mako holds the record for fastest swimming speed by a shark. One mako was clocked at more than forty miles per hour.

strongest bite:

Bull sharks have the greatest bite strength of any shark, even beating out the great white!

deadliest diet:

Hammerhead sharks may have the most dangerous eating habits of any shark. Stingrays, their favorite food, have sharp venomous spines on their tails. One hammerhead was found with nearly a hundred stingray spines in its mouth!

deepest diver:

The Portuguese dogfish has been found at depths of nearly ten thousand feet.

23

Shark Ancestors

Sharks have been around for approximately four hundred million years. That's two hundred million years before dinosaurs roamed the earth!

While some types of shark have survived millions of years, others have gone **extinct**.

Megalodon illustration

The largest shark that ever lived was the Megalodon. This prehistoric predator may have reached sixty feet in length.

fossilized Megalodon shark tooth and great white shark tooth

Scientists can tell a lot about the Megalodon from **fossil** evidence. Fossilized Megalodon teeth measuring up to seven inches high have been found.

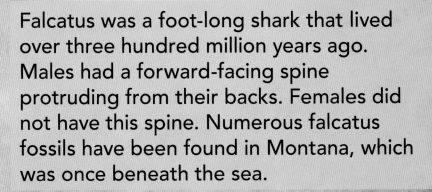
male falcatus fossil

Falcatus was a foot-long shark that lived over three hundred million years ago. Males had a forward-facing spine protruding from their backs. Females did not have this spine. Numerous falcatus fossils have been found in Montana, which was once beneath the sea.

? DID YOU KNOW? The oldest complete shark fossil found to date is over four hundred million years old. The ancient specimen of the *Doliodus problematicus*, a small shark measuring less than a foot in length, was found in New Brunswick, Canada.

shark fossil

Studying Sharks

Biologists have been using ROVs (remotely operated vehicles) for decades to get a better look at undersea life. ROVs can travel into waters that are too deep or dangerous for a human diver. In 2012, biologists using an ROV discovered a previously unknown shark species, the Galapagos catshark.

Despite using the latest technology to study sharks, there is still a lot to learn about these fascinating fish.

GPS (Global Positioning System) technology uses satellites to pinpoint locations anywhere on earth. Many cars are equipped with GPS devices, which help direct drivers to their destinations. Biologists are now using GPS on sharks!

A device containing a tiny transmitter is attached to the shark, allowing the shark's movements to be tracked. The data collected by these and other types of satellite tags help biologists learn more about shark behavior and migration patterns.

? DID YOU KNOW? You can go online to track the travel routes of tagged sharks. Some sharks even have their own Twitter accounts!

Threats to Sharks

Sharks play an important role in keeping our oceans healthy. When the top animal in a food chain disappears, its absence causes problems down the chain. If great white sharks were removed from an area, the number of seals (a favorite food item) would greatly increase. Too many hungry seals means not enough fish to go around. Eventually, the entire **ecosystem** would collapse.

What is the greatest threat to sharks? Humans. It is estimated that around one hundred million sharks are killed by humans each year.

Overfishing is the major cause of shark deaths each year. Because sharks grow slowly and only produce several young during their lifetime, more sharks are killed before they can grow their numbers.

One major cause of shark deaths is shark fin soup. Shark fin soup is a delicacy in parts of Asia. Fishermen catch sharks, cut off their fins, and throw their bodies back in the ocean. This is called finning.

To protect sharks from the practice of finning, the U.S. Congress passed the Shark Conservation Act in 2010. Several countries have banned shark fishing altogether.

Sharks! Quiz

1. Sharks are what type of animal?

    (a) Mammal
    (b) Fish
    (c) Whale
    (d) Amphibian

2. What shark can survive fresh water for long periods of time?

    (a) Tiger shark
    (b) Great white shark
    (c) Bull shark
    (d) Thresher shark

3. What causes shark skin to feel like sandpaper?

    (a) Dermal denticles
    (b) Barnacles
    (c) Algae
    (d) Hair

4. About how many teeth does a great white shark have in its mouth at all times?

    (a) 3,000
    (b) 150
    (c) 88
    (d) 1,237

5. Which is the largest shark?

   (a) Pygmy dogshark
   (b) Tiger Shark
   (c) Whale shark
   (d) Thresher shark

6. Which shark has an unusual head used to pin down prey?

   (a) Zebra shark
   (b) Hammerhead shark
   (c) Leopard shark
   (d) Bramble shark

7. What are photophores?

   (a) Tiny organisms that drift in the ocean
   (b) Spots on leopard sharks
   (c) Tiny organs that produce light
   (d) Remotely operated vehicles

8. What is the greatest threat to sharks?

   (a) Whales
   (b) Stingrays
   (c) Sea lions
   (d) Humans

Answers: 1. b 2. c 3. a 4. a 5. c 6. b 7. c 8. d

Glossary

apex predator an animal at the top of its food chain; no animals eat it

biologists people who study plants or animals

cartilage light, flexible material from which a shark's skeleton is made

dermal denticles tiny tooth-like structures covering a shark's skin

ecosystem a community of all the living things in an area

extinct a species that no longer exists

food chain the order that animals eat plants and other animals

fossil a trace or print or the remains of a plant or animal preserved in earth or rock

gills organs used by fish that allow them to breathe underwater

migrate to move across long distances